MANCHESTER DIALECT

A selection of words and anecdotes
from around Manchester

by
Camilla Brook-Chorlton

D1415945

BRADWELL
BOOKS

Published by Bradwell Books
9 Orgreave Close Sheffield S13 9NP
Email: books@bradwellbooks.co.uk

British Library Cataloguing in Publication Data:
a catalogue record for this book is available from the
British Library.

1st Edition

ISBN: 9781909914254

Print: Gomer Press, Llandysul, Ceredigion SA44 4JL

Artwork and design by: Andrew Caffrey
Photograph Shutterstock, Manchester Libraries and
Andy & Susan Caffrey

Introduction

'*Sorted*', '*Mad for it*', '*Banging*'... while the city of Manchester is known for its quirky language, it's all too easy to overlook the rich heritage of dialect and language throughout Greater Manchester. But look again and you'll see that there is a world of diverse dialect across the region. You only have to explore the astonishing number of dialect writers in the area's past to recognise this. From Urmston-born 'TIM BOBBIN', who was known as 'The Father of the Lancashire Dialect', to Rochdale's EDWIN WAUGH, known as the 'Prince of Dialect Poets', Greater Manchester's past is packed with people determined to bring its distinctive dialect to life.

In this book you'll discover the stories behind these often larger than life characters who counted caricaturist, print maker and political activist amongst their varied careers. You can also sample some of the works that earned these writers their fame, always improved by being read aloud to hear the dialect, of course. As you'll see in both these writings and those of other lesser-known Greater Manchester authors, it's not just the dialect but the humour which makes the dialect so special. Look at the dry wit of SKELTON'S '*Once I Wrote a Book*', for example, or the famous *Song of Solomon* in the Lancashire Accent, as spoken at Bolton. It is these poems and books which reveal just how closely dialect and place are connected. The wide range of writings from across Greater Manchester show the experience of life in Bolton, Salford, Rochdale and many other parts of Greater Manchester over one hundred years ago.

It's a colourful variety which continues to this day, as you'll see in the glossary which features familiar Manchester words as well as lesser-known ones. It would have been interesting to see what the dialect writers of the past would have thought when they heard people saying *'Salfords'*, *'Bang on'* or *'Bobbins'*!

While Cockney rhyming slang is well known across the world, we explore Manchester rhyming slang, an overlooked but no less entertaining phenomenon. Words can both obscure and reveal the secrets of the past, as we discover when exploring place names from across Greater Manchester. Could Wigan really have derived its name from a person called Wigan, and what is the truth behind Stockport's name?

The words that shape Greater Manchester continue to intrigue to this day. Enjoy your own journey through the region and its dialect.

Manchester dialect

Read on to explore words and sayings in use in different areas of Greater Manchester. From the very up to date to the more obscure, you can discover the meanings of words and phrases such as *'corporation pop'*, *'ginnel'* and *'jackbit'!* Greater Manchester's dialect is packed full of local words and sayings. As you'll see, some are remnants of its industrial past while others are rather more modern! There's no doubt that the city of Manchester and its surrounding areas have become associated with certain phrases which were brought to life in the 'Madchester' era. Manchester's dialect is so distinctive, there's even a BBC course that can help you learn to speak like a local!

Manchester Town Hall ©Andy & Susan Caffrey

Where did Greater Manchester's dialect come from?

There are many theories as to what inspired the dialects throughout Greater Manchester. While Greater Manchester is its own place now and no longer part of the county of Lancashire, it is possible to detect more than a hint of the language of the old Lancashire people in its dialects and accents. The local dialect is also believed to have been enriched by the many immigrants who became part of the region's history over the years. Whatever the influences on its dialect, Manchester's celebrities and cultural figures have helped to keep it in the public eye and, as you'll see, lots of these words and phrases have gone into common use in other parts of the country. But even within one area such as Greater Manchester, word meanings can become complex. In another part of this book, we explore the subtleties of talking about bread when you're in the region!

Manchester Libraries

Glossary

A

Ace – very good

Alleys and dobbers – marbles

Alright? – how are you?

'Angin' – (Hanging) disgusting, not nice

Ann Twacky (or ann twacky) – old-fashioned

'Ave a word – to have a talk with someone

B

Babbiesyed – meat pie on a muffin

Bang on – perfect

Bap – bread roll

Barm – bread roll

Barmy – mad/eccentric

Barney – argument

Belting – great

Bessies – best friends

Bins – spectacles

Blimey! – exclamation of amazement

Blinder – something great

Blinding – very good

Bloke – man

Blud – friend/brother

Bobbins – rubbish/not good

Bob off – to leave

Bobby – police officer

Bog – toilet

Bonce – head

Booze – alcoholic drink

Brew – hill

C

Cabbaged – confused, messed up

Champion – good

Charabang – a coach

Cheers – thank you

Chill out – relax

Chillin' – relaxing

Chip muffin – chip butty

Chilly – cold

Chinwag – chat

Chippy – fish and chip shop

Chuck it – throw it away

Chuddy/chud – chewing gum

Chuffed – very pleased, happy

Closet – toilet

Cob – bread roll

Cock – mate or friend
Copper – police officer

D

Daft 'apeth – fool, idiot
Dead – very, extremely
Deaking – looking
Dibble – the police
Digits – number
Dope – really good
Drizzle – light rain
Dry – boring

Manchester Libraries

E

Epic – good

F

Fettle – fix or repair

G

Gaff – home

Gaggin' – very thirsty

Gigs – glasses

Ginnel – alleyway through a row of houses

Gob – mouth

Gonk – idiot

Gormless – stupid

Grand – very good

Gravy – good

Gump – foolish person

Gutted – upset, disappointed

H

Heads – people

Hiya – hello

Hotpot – stew

I

Innit? – isn't it?

J

Jackbit – food
Jiggered – tired out

K

Keks – trousers
Kippered – tired
Knackered – tired

L

Lad – boy/man
Ladged – embarrassed
Lanry – bleach
Lass – girl
Later(s) – goodbye
Lobby – hall (as in entrance)
Lothered – sweating

Lozz – to lie about lazily

M

Madchester – the alternative name for Manchester which developed around its vibrant music scene in the late 1980s and early 1990s

Made up – really happy

Madhead – crazy person

Mad hot – very hot

Mad keen – very enthusiastic

Manny – local name for Manchester

Mardy – bad tempered

Mate – friend

Mint – great, very good

Minging – unclean/unattractive

Mingey – mean

Mither – bother, trouble

N

Napper – head

Newtons – teeth

Nice one/top one – very good

Nippers – young kids

Nowt – nothing

Nowty – grumpy

Numpty – idiot, stupid person

O

Owt – anything

P

Pal – friend

Peeps – people

Peppered – broke

Petty – toilet

Pog – to steal

Pop – fizzy drink

Poorly – unwell

Potato hash – mashed potato and meat

Potty – mad/eccentric

Pow – haircut

Proper – very

Pure – really good

R

Ragged – messy

Raz – something's good/great

Right – very
Round of toast – a slice of toast
Rozzer – police officer

S

Safe – OK
Salfords – socks
Sarnie – sandwich
Schnoz – nose
Scran – food
Scrikin' – crying
Shickers – beers
Sick – good/fantastic
Sis – sister
Sken – look
Skrieking – crying
Slopstone – sink
Smokin' – good
Smuv – winter coat
Snide – mean
Soft – silly, stupid
Sound – good or decent
Sorted! – great, all set up
Strop – tantrum
Spanner – a daft person

Spitting – raining lightly
Spuds – potatoes
Summat – something

T

Tenner – ten-pound note
Tilly – area near the back door where mop was kept
Top – good
Trolleys – trousers, underwear
Turn it in – stop it
Tutty – lipstick, make-up

V

Varnyear – nearly

W

Wupding – someone who is not very bright

Y

Yard – house
Yoghurt – a person with a confused view of life, or differing views to your own

Sayings

'My stomach thinks my throat's been cut!' –
  I'm feeling very hungry!

'Fish, chips and peas with pea wet' –
  Fish, chips and peas with the water they were cooked in

'What did they cut your hair with, a knife and fork?' –
  You have a dodgy haircut!

'Nah man' – I don't believe that!

'Swear down' – I'm telling the truth!

'Our kid' – Close friend or sibling

'You don't get owt for nowt' –
  You can't get something for nothing!

'Give your 'ead a wobble' – You need to have a rethink

'You're peckin' me 'ead' – You're annoying me

'Stop ya chattin' – Stop talking a load of rubbish!

'Ave it!' – An exclamation of celebration,
  usually after a success

'Mind out!' – Be careful!

'Let's crack on' – Let's get on with it

'Get lost!' – Go away!

'Give over!' – Stop it

'In a bit!' – Soon, bye

'Put wood int 'ole.' – Shut the door

'My gaff' – My house

'Mad for it' – Overexcited, very happy

'Sat here like piffy on a rock' –
    Sitting waiting around for someone to arrive

'He couldn't stop a pig in a ginnel' – He has bandy legs

'Your hair is full o' lugs' – Your hair is very knotted

'That is bobbins' – That's not very good

'That is well bad' – That's a bad situation

'Going off' – Out of control

'Dicky Mint' – A little bit strange

'Corporation pop' – Water

'Chip off' – To leave

'Bob on!' – That's correct!

'Down our end' – Where we live

'Go on a mooch' – Go on a long walk
    for no particular reason

'Go on a trek/mission' – Go on a really long walk
    for a reason

'I'm sweating cobs' – I'm really hot

'I haven't the foggiest' – I have no idea

'It was a piece of cake' – It was very easy

'Get yer mad up' – Become angry

'Y' all right?' – How are you?

'Yer fibbin'!' – You're lying

'You barmy dog!' – You're very silly

'What it is, right …' – I'm about to explain
    something to you

'Nah man' – No way

'Get off and milk it' – Derogatory greeting for cyclists

'Gotta chip. It's hair-washing time' – It's time
for me to leave

'Out of order' – Not right

'Bang out of order' – Not right at all

'Playing Walley' – Kicking a football against the wall

'I'm 'avin' that/it' – I like that a lot

'Use your swede!' – Use your head!

'You're shredding my swede!' – You're being very annoying!

'Telling chinnies' – Telling lies

'On't cod.' – I'm only joking

'Alreet?' – How are you?

'Not t'neet' – Not this evening

'Lothert!' – I'm very warm

'Pots fer rags' – Silly

'Our kid' – Brother

'Old fella' – Dad

'Do you need a lift with that?' – Do you need
a hand with that?

'What are you skenning at?' – What are you looking at?

'Mee-maw' – To communicate with a person using a
combination of exaggerated facial expressions, sign
language and lip reading. This expression apparently
refers to the way that mill workers communicated with
each other over the noise of the machinery during the
industrial revolution.

Greater Manchester born and bread

Watch out when you get hungry in Greater Manchester. You might need to have a think before you ask for a humble sandwich. This is because the area has many different terms for a breadcake! Travel around different areas of Greater Manchester and you'll discover many words for what is essentially the same thing. These include *bap*, *barm*, *barmcake*, *breadcake*, *flourcake*, *teacake* and *muffin!*

The humble chip barm Shutterstock/Crepesoles

A little word about rhyming slang

We've all heard of Cockney rhyming slang, but what about Greater Manchester rhyming slang? Yes, Manchester has its own version of the cryptic language. Similar to Cockney rhyming slang, Greater Manchester slang applies part of a phrase or a couple of words that rhyme with the word to which you're referring. The alternative words used give an interesting insight into the history of the saying and the area, for example 'bobbins' perhaps refers to the region's industrial past.

Lancashire Cotton Mill Shutterstock/George Green

Bartons – socks (from Barton Docks)

Bells – fingers (from bell ringers)

Bobbins – rotten (from bobbins of cotton)

Claires – trainers (from Claire Rayners)

Gorton – bank (from Gorton Tank)

Newtons – teeth (from Newton Heath)

Orange – wash (from orange squash)

Salfords – socks (from Salford Docks)

Standat – cheese (from 'stand at ease' – a military term)
Traff – any person called Mark (from Trafford Park)
Whalley – change/loose change (from Whalley Range)

What's in a name?

Greater Manchester's place names may be familiar, but what actually lies behind them? What do they reveal about the past? Read on to find out more…

WIGAN

The last remaining vintage windmill in Greater Manchester
Shutterstock/Eddie J. Rodriquez

Wigan is thought to be a very old name, going all the way back to the seventh century. Believed to mean 'village', it is thought that Wigan is actually named after a person called Wigan! Its names are also recorded as being Wygayn and Wygan. Another interpretation of the name is that it actually refers to a local Rowan tree or 'Wiggin Tree'. However, Wigan was known by another name back in the nineteenth century. Thanks to its significant part in the Industrial Revolution, Wigan was referred to as 'Coalopolis'.

Just don't get confused if you hear a reference to 'Wigan Pier'. It doesn't mean that the place has a secret seaside tucked away. It was George Formby who joked that Wigan had a pier. In reality, Wigan Pier now refers to an area of warehouses on the Leeds and Liverpool Canal.

BOLTON

The place name Bolton is thought to be derived from Bothl-tun, which is an Old English word meaning 'a settlement complete with dwelling'. It is believed that the first recorded use of the name – Boelton – used to refer to Bolton le Moors. Various versions are recorded throughout the years. There's a neat tie-in between Bolton's name and its motto. This is because supera moras (overcome difficulties) is derived from a pun on the version of the place name which is Bolton-super-Moras. Translated literally, this means Bolton on the Moors.

BURY

Bury's name refers to its past identity as a stronghold, fort or borough because that is what the early versions of the name (Byri or Buri) mean in Old English.

ROCHDALE

The historic Rochdale canal Shutterstock/Marbury

Rochdale's location on the River Roch is thought to have given it its name. But earlier versions of the name suggest that Rochdale may have first taken its name from a word meaning 'hall'.

OLDHAM

Oldham's name is an interesting one which has inspired plenty of debate about whether it is derived from Saxon or Old Norse. Does it hark back to a Norse word which means 'outcrop' or is it derived from the Saxon word for 'old village or place'? It is even thought that the name may refer to an outcrop belonging to a farmer called Alda! Whatever the truth, local people have their own affectionate pronunciation for the name of their home town: 'Owdom'.

TAMESIDE

Tameside's history is a complex one because it has only been a metropolitan borough since 1974, though it is an area with a rich heritage. Naming the new borough was a challenging process. With so many towns involved in naming it, consensus was difficult to come by! The various suggestions included Ninetowns, West Pennine, Kayborough and Brigantia.

STOCKPORT

Stockport's name is thought to have been constructed from two Saxon words: the first is 'stock' (meaning a castle or

Oldham - circa 1898 Shutterstock/Elzbieta Sekowska

stockade place) and the second is 'port' (which means a castle within a wood). With Stockport in possession of its own fine motte and bailey castle back in the 1100s, there are no prizes for guessing which castle the name refers to! However, there is another interpretation of the name which is that back in the Saxon times when it was a small village, it was called Stockport, which means 'the market place at the hamlet'.

Old Market place in Stockport Shutterstock/Tupungato

MANCHESTER

Manchester is a familiar name throughout the world, but from where does the city actually derive its name? According to Oxford University Press, the city takes its name from the term 'Mamucium' which was the Roman name for a first-century settlement and fort built there in AD79.

Roman remains in Manchester ©Andy & Sue Caffrey

TRAFFORD

Along with Tameside, Trafford is one of the two Greater Manchester boroughs which is not based around a town or city. In fact, Trafford has only existed as a metropolitan borough since 1974. Again, there was some debate about an appropriate name for the new borough, whether it should be Watlingford, Crossford or something else. Trafford was seen as the best choice because it brought together many links with the area's past and present, such as Old Trafford, Trafford Park and the de Trafford family, an ancient land-owning family based in the area for many years.

SALFORD

Salford's name is thought to provide a poetic reference to its past. This is because the Old English version of the name refers to a ford located by the willow trees which grew along the River Irwell.

30

Salford Quays Shutterstock/Steve Allen

Greater Manchester:

Domain of the dialect writers

Greater Manchester is fortunate in having had its distinctive dialect recorded by a succession of writers. These individuals caught the language and the voice of their day by capturing it phonetically and bringing their local dialect to life through songs and poems. They were so prolific that a monument was created to mark the achievements of some of them at the Lancashire Dialect Writers' Memorial in Bradfield Park in Rochdale.

From The Writings of OLIVER ORMEROD, with a memoir of the author by H.V COLLEY MARCH

On the 27th October, 1900, the Dialect Writers Memorial, erected on the Rochdale Park Slopes, was unveiled. It bears the bronze medallion-effigies of Edwin Waugh, Oliver Ormerod, John Trafford Clegg and Margaret Rebecca Lahee; the dates of birth and death of each, and a typical quotation from their folk-speech. But that of others ought not to be quite forgotten; of John Collier, John Byrom, Samuel Laycock, and Ben Brierley.

Inscription on the Rochdale Writers' Memorial

In grateful memory of the four Rochdale writers of the Lancashire dialect who have preserved for our children in verse and prose that

will not die, the strength and tenderness, the gravity and humours
of the folk of our day, in the tongue and talk of the people. This
memorial was erected A.D. 1900

Read on to discover a little of these writers and their
writings. Try reading the excerpts out loud – it may help
you to discover more of the dialect that these local authors
worked so hard to capture!

Dialect Writers'
Memorial in
Rochdale
Creative Commons

'TIM BOBBIN': 'The Father of the Lancashire Dialect'

John Collier
Creative Commons

TIM BOBBIN was the pseudonym of JOHN COLLIER. Born in Urmston, Trafford, Collier wrote extensively in his local dialect. Probably his best-known work is *A View of the Lancashire Dialect; containing the Adventures and Misfortunes of a Lancashire Clown by Tim Bobbin*. Published in 1750, the book is a comic dialogue between two characters, Thomas and Mary. It also provides a detailed glossary of Lancashire words and phrases collected over many years. But it was a book published in 1850 which brought Collier even more fame and fortune. This was the somewhat wordily titled *Tim Bobbin's Tummus and Meary; with His Rhymes and an Enlarged and Amended Glossary of Words and Phrases, Chiefly Used by the Rural Population of the Manufacturing Districts of South Lancashire*. It was the first attempt at creating a scientific survey of the

Lancashire dialect, earning Collier the grand title of 'the Father of Lancashire Dialect'. It went on to significantly influence many other local writers. An eccentric character, when he wasn't writing, playing music or working in his day job as the master of a village school, Collier was fond of – and famed for – creating wicked caricatures, for which he was given the name 'the Lancashire Hogarth'.

From Memoir of JOHN COLLIER
From TIM BOBBIN'S Tummus and Meary

Several writers have endeavoured, both in prose and rhyme, to express themselves in the Lancashire dialect, but, with one or two exceptions, they have not succeeded. The fact is, that until the present edition, there has not been any true glossary to write the dialect by, that of Tim Bobbin, if truth may be stated, being itself far from correct. I may be blamed by some, for being thus candid, but the fact had often been forced on my attention, both from my own observation and that of others … His Lancashire Dialect was not the spoken dialect of any one district of the county; and his friend Mr. Townley, of Belfield, in writing to a gentleman at Manchester, describes him as taking note of every quaint, odd, out of the way term, or phrase, which he heard during his perambulations in different parts of the country, and incorporating them in his *View of the Lancashire Dialect*.

WILLIAM HARRISON AINSWORTH

'She would rather be an old man's darling than a young man's warling.'
WILLIAM HARRISON AINSWORTH

Born in 1805 in Manchester, Ainsworth became a popular romantic novelist. He published his first two novels, *Sir John Chiverton* and *Rookwood*, in 1826 and 1834 respectively. He then went on to produce no fewer than 40 historical romances! Many of his books feature local dialects. Some of his best-known works are *Old St Paul's*, *Windsor Castle* and *The Lancashire Witches*, an excerpt from which you can read below.

From *The Lancashire Witches: A Romance of Pendle Forest*, published in 1849

For a while the abbot remained shattered and stupefied by this terrible interview. At length, he arose, and made his way, he scarce knew how, to the oratory. But it was long before the tumult of his thoughts could be at all allayed, and he had only just regained something like composure when he was disturbed by hearing a slight sound in the adjoining chamber. A mortal chill came over him, for he thought it might be Demdike returned. Presently, he distinguished a footstep stealthily approaching him, and almost hoped that the wizard would consummate his vengeance by taking his life. But he was quickly undeceived, for a hand was placed on his shoulder, and a friendly voice whispered in his ears, 'Cum along wi' meh , lort abbut. Get up , quick – quick!'

Thus addressed, the abbot raised his eyes, and beheld a rustic figure standing beside him, divested of his clouted shoes, and armed with a long bare wood-knife.

'Dunna yo knoa me, lort abbut?' cried the person. 'Ey'm a freent – Hal o' Nabs, o' Wiswall. Yo'n moind Wiswall, yeawr own birthplace, abbut? Dunna be feert, ey sey. Ey'n getten a steeigh clapt to yon windaw , an' you con be down it i' a trice – an' along t' covert way be t' river soide to t' mill.'

But the abbot stirred not.

'Quick! quick!' implored Ha; o' Nabs, venturing to pluck the abbot's sleeve. 'Every minute 's precious. Dunna be feert. Ebil Croft, t' miller is below. Poor Cuthbert Ashbead would ha' been here i'stead o' meh 'if he couldn; boh that accursed wizard, Nick Demdike, tumed my hont agen him, and drove t' poike head intended for himself into poor Cuthbert's side. They clapt meh i' a dungeon, boh Ebil monaged to get me out, an' ey then swore to do whot poor Cuthbert would ha' done, if he'd been livin' – so here ey am, lort abbut , cum to set yo free. An neaw yo knoan aw abowt it, yo con ha nah more hesitation. Cum, time presses, ah ey'm feert o' t' guard owerhearing us.'

'I thank you, my good friend, from the bottom of my heart,' replied the abbot, rising; 'but, however strong may be the temptation of life and liberty which you hold out to me , I cannot yield to it. I have pledged my word to the Earl of Derby to make no attempt to escape. Were the doors thrown open, and the guard removed, I should remain where l am.'

Pendle Hill Shutterstock/Jane McIlroy

SAMUEL BAMFORD

Manchester Libraries

Born in 1788 in the village of Middleton, Rochdale, SAMUEL BAMFORD went on to become a high-profile radical and writer. Starting out as a weaver and a warehouseman, Bamford became involved in political activities and was a poet and a journalist. His political views inspired and shaped his writings and he wrote in standard English as well as in the Lancashire dialect. Bamford's works include *Passages in the Life of a Radical* (for which he is best known today), *Walks Among the Workers of the Cotton Districts* and *Walks in South Lancashire*. As he grew in political awareness, he became increasingly interested in dialect literature and was sometimes seen at the meetings of the Sun Inn circle of Lancashire poets and authors in Manchester. This interest evolved into a glossary of the Lancashire dialect, produced with WILLIAM GASKELL and the Manchester Literary and Philosophical Society. First published in 1850, this glossary became the basis for future Lancashire dialect dictionaries.

In the first of Bamford's poems as you can see in the excerpt on the page opposite, Bamford refers directly to TIM BOBBIN, the 'Father of the Lancashire Dialect.'

From *Homely Rhymes, Poems and Reminiscences,* published in 1864

Tim Bobbin's Grave

Awe stoode beside Tim Bobbin's grave
'At looks o'er Ratchda' teawn;
An th' owd lad woke within his yerth,
An' sed, 'Wheer arto' beawn?'

''Awm gooin' into th' Packer-street,
As far as th' Gowden Bell,
To taste o' Daniel's Kesmus ale.'
Tim — 'I cud like o saup mysel'.

''An' by this hont o' my reet arm,
If fro' that hole theaw'll reawk,
Theaw'st have o saup o'th' best breawn ale
'At ever lips did seawk.'

The greawnd it sturr'd beneath my feet,
An' then I yerd a groan;
He shook the dust fro' off his skull,
An' rowlt away the stone.

I brought him op a deep breawn jug,
'At o gallon did contain;
An' he took it at one blessed draught,
An laid him deawn again!

Song – The Gonnor
A Gonnor dwells o' th' Barrowfells,
O, he's a meety gonnor:
Of gonnors o', he bears the bells,
An' surely that's a honour;
Some time ago, as yo' mun kno',
Authority wur gin him,
To banish ducks, fro' dams an brucks,
If after daylit swimmin

As looks 'a gentleman o'th' teawn,'
When stufft wi' public dinner,
Upon a cholic grip'n cleawn,
A hungry, wand'rin sinner;
As looks at my poor rhymin ripp
A welkin-born Pegasus;
So awful looks his gonnorship,
As o'er the wave he passes.
He chanc't to look into a nook,
An' theer espy'd wi pleasure,
Some duckys bent o' merriment,

Just tipplin' at their leisure;
Then swell'd his breast, an' he his crest
Tow'rd heaven he distended;
An deep he swore, by flood an shore,
Their manners shud be mended.
Neaw ducks, yo' known, cry quack, quack, quack,
An geese dun hiss and cackle,
An this, a tawkin' is their mack,
When they'n a mind to rattle:
So, void of grace, wi' brazent face
He in goose-language tow'd 'em,
'At he durst swear, by th' book o' prayer,
They'rn nowty ducks fro' Owdham.

MARGARET LAHEE

When we lay deaun life's shuttle an' stone before the greyt judge,
He'll wont to know what sooat of a piece we'n woven,
An how many floats there's in it,
He winnot care abeawt eawr hee seaundin' names an' worldly
possessions.
He'll ax us how we got em an what we did wi' em.

MARGARET REBECCA LAHEE, as quoted on the Lancashire
Dialect Writers' Memorial in Bradfield Park, Rochdale.

While she was actually born in Carlow, Ireland in 1831,

MARGARET LAHEE spent a great deal of her life in Rochdale. She became involved in capturing the local dialect through writing and went on to became one of only a very small number of female dialect writers of the 1800s to have her work published.

EDWIN WAUGH

Manchester Libraries

If a man was a pair of steam-looms, how carefully would he be oiled, and tended, and mended, and made to do all that a pair of looms could do. What a loom, full of miraculous faculties, is he compared to these – the master-piece of nature for creative power and for wonderful variety of excellent capabilities! Yet, with what a profuse neglect he is cast away, like the cheapest rubbish on the earth!

Known as the 'Prince of Dialect Poets' and a true champion of the Lancashire dialect, EDWIN WAUGH was born in Rochdale in 1817.

In 1855, he published his first book, *Sketches of Lancashire Life and Localities*. But it was in 1856 that he published his dialect poem, *'Come whoam to thi childer an' me'*. Waugh is now commemorated on the Lancashire Dialect Writers' Memorial in Rochdale.

From *Folk songs and folk-speech of Lancashire: on the ballads and songs of the county Palatine* by WILLIAM E.A. AXON, published 1871

'Of the dialect, Mr. Waugh was the first who painted at full length, with all its lights and shades, the portrait of a Lancashire lad. He thus opened a vein of considerable richness, and although many have followed in his footsteps none have surpassed him. The pathos and simplicity of his now famous lyric 'Come Whoam to thi Childher an Me' at once gave him the place as the laureate of Lancashire; and a succession of charming songs, some of which, in beauty, far excel that maiden effort bear witness to his dramatic power, and his ability to link together beauty of thought and language "in lengthened sweetness, long drawn out".

'Mr. Waugh was born at Rochdale in 1819, and is a self-educated man. In his youth and early manhood he was engaged as a journeyman printer. During the existence of the National School Association, he was one of its secretaries, and since then has chiefly devoted himself to literature. His philosophy is of the genial order, he is no lachrymose

sage running hither and thither, and crying woe, woe, but one loving
the sunny side of things, blessed with a keen enjoyment of life, a vivid
perception of the beauty of nature, and deriving from it compensation
for the crosses of life. The dignity and nobility of labour, the sacredness
of duty, the claims of home and family, of brotherhood and humanity
are the chief doctrines in his creed.'

From *Poems and Lancashire Songs* by EDWIN WAUGH

Come Whoam To Thy Childer an' Me

Aw've just mended th' fire wi' a cob;
Owd Swaddle has brought thi new shoon;
There's some nice bacon-collops o'th hob
An' a quart o' ale posset i'th oon;
Aw've brought thi top-cwot, doesto know
For th'rain's comin' deawn very dree;
An th' har'stone's as white as new snow;–
Come whoam to thi childer an' me

When aw put little Sally to bed,
Hoo cried 'cose her feyther weren't theer,
So aw kiss'd th' little thing, an aw said
Thae'd bring her a ribbon fro' th' fair;
An' aw gave her a doll, an some rags
An' a nice little white cotton-bo';
An' aw kiss'd her again; but hoo said

'At hoo wanted to kiss thee an' o'

An' Dick, too, aw'd sich wark wi' him,
Afore aw could get him up stairs;
Thae towd him thae'd bring him a drum,
He said, when he're sayin his prayers
Then he looked i' my face, an' he said,
'Has th' boggarts taen houd o' my dad?'
An' he cried till his e'en were quite red;–
He likes thee some weel, does yon lad!

At th' lung-length, aw geet 'em laid still;
An' aw hearken't folks' feet 'at went by;
So aw iron't o' my clooas reet well,
An' aw hanged 'em o'th maiden to dry;
When aw'd mended thi stockin's an' shirts,
Aw sit deawn to knit i' my cheer,
An' aw rayley did feel rayther hurt,–
Mon, aw'm one-ly when theaw arrn't theer.

'Aw've a drum an' a trumpet for Dick;
Aw've a yard o' blue ribbon for Sal;
Aw've a book full o' babs, an' a stick
An' some 'bacco an' pipes for mysel';
Aw've brought thee some coffee an' tay,–
Iv thae'll feel i' my pocket, tha'll see;

An' aw've bought tho a new cap to-day,–
But Aw al'ays brings summat for thee!

'God bless tho', my lass; aw'll go whoam,
An' aw'll kiss the an' th' childer o' round;
Thae knows, that wherever aw roam,
Aw'm fain to get back to th' owd ground;
Aw can do wi' a crack o'er a glass;
Aw can do wi' a bit of a spree;
But aw've no gradely comfort, my lass,
Except wi' yon childer and thee.'

From Lancashire Songs by Edwin Waugh

Come, Mary, link thi arm i' mine

Come, Mary, link thi arm i' mine,
An' lilt away wi' me;
An' dry that little drop o' brine.
Fro' th' corner o' thi e'e;
Th' momin' dew i'th' heather-bell's
A bonny gem o' weet;
That tear a different story tells, –
It pains my heart to see't.
So, Mary, link thi arm i' mine.

No lordly ho' o' th' country-side's

So welcome to my view,
As th' little cottage where abides
My sweetheart, kind an' true;
But, there's a nook beside yon spring,
An' iv thae'll share't wi' me;
Aw'll buy tho th' prattist gowden ring
That ever theaw did see !
So, Mary, link thi arm i' mine.

My feyther's gan mo forty peawnd,
I' silver an' i' gowd;
An' a bonny bit o' garden greawnd,
O'th' mornin' side o' th' fowd;
An' a honsome bible, clen an' new.
To read for days to come; –
There's leaves for writin' names in, too,
Like th' owd un at's awhoam.
So, Mary, link thi arm i' mine.

JOHN TRAFFORD CLEGG

JOHN TRAFFORD CLEGG was another Greater Manchester writer who went on to be celebrated on the Lancashire Dialect Writers' Memorial in Rochdale. Born in 1857 in Milnrow, Clegg only lived to the age of 38. Yet he became part of the tradition of dialect writers in the region, inspired by his work as a typesetter to craft sketches and tales of local life in Rochdale. In the second excerpt below, Clegg refers to the ancient Lancashire tradition of pace egging.

From *The Works of John Trafford Clegg*, published 1895

From the Introduction

His work in the dialect met with unqualified praise from critics, who were unanimous in their opinions of its merit. Such high-class journals as the London Morning Post, and Lloyds News, and several of the leading literary journals, gave most highly favourable notices of his first publication, 'Reaund bi th' Derby'; and the Saturday Review had the following appreciative criticism, which is the highest testimony to the author's abilities:

'The author is a Rochdale man, and an acute observer of the humours of Lancashire weavers. His descriptions of rambles about the country, possess the best qualities of sketches. They are full of brightness and life. His verse, too, shows other gifts of the poet than the mere accomplishment of rhyming.'

This high character is maintained through all the author's productions in the dialect. The scenes are mostly in the neighbourhood of Rochdale, but occasionally the author has travelled farther afield.

Bowd Slasher

It's a good while sin' aw went a pace-eggin mysel, neaw, but aw'm olez intherested i' t' Good Friday performances o' th' owd play. Who wrote that stirrin thragedy, aw wondher? It's bin honded deawn moore bi word o' meauth nor printin, aw think, as far as Rachda gwoes, shuzheaw; for yo'll have a job to find two books alike, or ony book where it's set deawn same as t' lads play it.

There's good points abeaut t' thing. Every acthor gets summat to do an' say: there's no supers, abeaut, an' nobry maudlin reaund th' stage to put time on. Then, every mon tells his name an' business when he first comes in; a first-rate plan, savin a dyel o' bother an' study for onybody 'at stons hearkenin. There's no women i' t'road, noather, nobbut Dirty Bet, an' hoo doesn't ceaunt; so t' chaps con get forrad wi their wark in a business-like style, an' feight away beaut onybody meddlin wi em. Th' action never stops, for every scene's a feight in it, an' th' excitement keeps grooin whol Bet comes in wi her besom to sweep up for a finish.

An' what grand characthers they are !

OLIVER ORMEROD

OLIVER ORMEROD is also featured on Rochdale's Dialect Writers' Memorial. Born in Rochdale in 1811, Ormerod was a radical as well as a writer and a keen keeper of his local dialect.

From *Writings* by OLIVER ORMEROD, HENRY COLLEY MARCH, published 1901

Introduction

Half-a-century has elapsed since the publication of a pamphlet written in the vernacular Rochdale Dialect served to extend the fame of OLIVER ORMEROD beyond his native town. Locally entitled 'The Felley fro Rachde' it describes the impressions of a shrewd Lancashire lad on his first visit to the metropolis and the Great Exhibition of 1851. The popularity of this brochure, original in its conception and racy of the soil, was immediate and great. The First and Second Editions consisting of 7,000 copies, the Author says 'sowd like winkin'.

Chapter One

To maw thynkin evury mon us con foind toime un brass, shud neaw un then goo fro whome, fur iv o mon keawurs deawn uv his oan durstoane O his loive, E dusent kno naut o wat's gooin on in his oan nativ lond, heaw con E? Un ut tis presunt toime to maw thynkin, aw'd eldur goo fur o sodier, nur olis stop wheere aw wur bom, just mete saime us o moile stoane ur o turmit. Wen o mon's bin o travillur, un ad o deyle o diskoarse we his felley kraturs, E con goo hinto ony mak o kumpany us E appens fur to be ax'd fur to goo hinto, beawt lookin sich o foo. It mays his moind grew biggur, un saime toime iv it wor fur to grew biggur evury day, E nevur

needs his clewus lettin eawt. Us soune as aw yerd uth Krystil
Palus, un wat foke sed us ud bin theere, thynks aw to mesel, 'that's
the ticket,' un aw startud o studyin obeawt it, un ofore lung aw
'greed wi mesel us aw'd goo, othur be hooke ur be krooke. Aw'd saift
o bit o brass, un we that aw'd no sanner komn too o konklushun fur
to goo, nur aw wor welley reddy fur to 'kut me blessed stik'. Iv aw'd
had no brass, aw'd nevur o dun us aw bin towd o deyle o chaps han
dun. Waw! they sen us mony o won us popt bwoth watchus un
clewus o purpus fur to raze brass fur to goo we.

BENJAMIN BRIERLEY

BENJAMIN BRIERLEY (or BEN BRIERLEY, as he was often known
in his time) did not start out as a writer. Born in 1825 in
Failsworth near Oldham, he worked as a weaver in a textile
factory. It was once he started sending articles to the local
papers that his work gained public acclaim.

From *Tales and Sketches of Lancashire Life* by BEN BRIERLEY,
published 1884

Putting on his hat, and taking his stick out of its corner, he made
another journey to the door.

'I'st be back before thou's done smoothin,' he said to the daughter,
who did not appear to have the slightest objection to his going
out. 'Mak me a bit o' posset, and put it i'th' oon again I come.

Dunno' mak it too sweet; un' mind it isno' lumpy. Thou may gratter a bit o' nutmeg in it, just for a change. See ut th' sheets are weel aired, an' draw th' curtains nicely round th' bed, but not too close. Now, then.'

After delivering himself of these instructions, old Makapenny closed the door, banged the gate, and shambled down to the 'Jolly Carter'. Instead of finding a room full of company, as he had expected, the retired grocer met with no one at the tavern, except a solitary stranger, who sat blinking his eyes at the fire, and nursing the remnant of a 'gill' that appeared to have forgotten when it was drawn. This stranger was a man apparently much older than himself, with long flowing white hair, white furry eyebrows, a beard that was marvellously fine and woolly, and a form that was surprisingly erect for his age. He appeared not to notice old Makapenny as the latter entered; but sat with his back partially turned towards him, and his eyes still intent upon the 'rack-an'-hook' hanging in the chimney. He was respectably, if not well dressed, Makapenny observed, surveying the stranger from head to foot.

From *Treadlepin Fold*, published 1884

Ned was busy repairing the embankment of an artificial duckpond which he had constructed in one corner of the house by damming up with moist clay a space extending from the window to the chimney, and filling it with water.

One of the children, who, it appeared, had a taste for aquatics, and had no doubt been an adept at sink navigation, had bored a hole through the clay, through which the water had emptied itself, much to the chagrin of Ned and the discomfiture of the astonished ducks. The head of the family raised himself from his position as soon as he saw his companion, who was leaning against the 'speer', and drawing his sleeve across his upper lips, bade him 'Good mornin'.

'Thou sees,' he remarked, 'what it is t' have a pa'cel o' childer ut are aulus i' some sort o' mischief. I but made this hole o' th' beginnin o' last week, an' as soon as I filled it in! Wayther our Jack keawert (sat) hissel down in it; an' t'other day our Bob threw a chicken into 't, an welly nee drownt it; an' now our Bill has gone an letten it off – little pousement! But let me catch any on 'em about it again,' he continued, looking threateningly towards the table; 'I'll pound 'em they'n ha' t' go beaut porritch for once.'

The little group to whom the last words were addressed lowered their eyes and looked solemn at this, and the looks of the father were as anxiously watched as though the promised visitation was actually impending. Ned, as soon as he had washed his hands, seated himself at the table, along with his wife, and invited his friend to a chair which stood in the opposite nook; then, seizing a spoon with a wooden handle and poising it over the dish, gave

the signal, 'looad!' A sheaf of spoons simultaneously clattered into
the dish at this invitation. The steam broke out afresh in a denser
cloud, and the splashing and blubbering which followed showed that
business was going on in first-rate style. Owd Linderinbant, though
necessarily absorbed in his own immediate speculations, could not
help taking a more than usual interest in the work that was going on
at the table. How happy the whole jorum appeared to be!'

Sound familiar?

Greater Manchester's past and present is packed full of
familiar names and some more unusual ones, too.

WIGAN

Did you know that Wigan people are known as pie eaters?
No, that isn't a rude comment on their eating habits. The
nickname is thought to go back to the days of the 1926
General Strike. During this time, miners in Wigan were
forced back into work due to a lack of food. This history
is now celebrated today in a light-hearted way with the
World Pie Eating Championship which has taken place in
Wigan every year since 1992. But pie isn't the only food
for which Wigan is famous. If you've ever had beans on
toast, the chances are that you've enjoyed Heinz beans, as
processed and packaged in Wigan at **H. J. HEINZ**, Wigan
which is not only the largest food processing plant in

Europe, but the largest Heinz facility in the world! Wigan was also the birthplace of the hugely successful Indian food company, **PATAK'S**.

BOLTON

Bolton Town Hall Shutterstock/Eddie J. Rodriquez

Have you ever had an ice cream sandwich? Then you have an ice cream seller named Lewis from Bolton to thank. It was he who, while working on his market stall in Bolton Market Hall, thought up a clever brass slide for making a portion of ice cream to fit new wafer biscuits! Clever. Thanks to the way they were made, these inventions were first known as 'sliders'. Bolton's history features daily necessities as well as sweet treats as it is the home of British baking brand, **WARBURTONS**. **WARBURTONS** was quite literally 'raised' from its humble beginnings in a grocery shop in Bolton in 1876 to become one of the most recognised brands on the bakery shelf.

Think of big names in sportswear and you'll probably think of brands that are not only popular with world-class players, but also sought after by famous (and sometimes infamous) celebrities. It would all have been most surprising to JOSEPH WILLIAM FOSTER in Holcombe Brook, just a few miles outside Bolton. After all, he just had the idea of creating a spiked running shoe as part of the range of everyday running shoes that he sold. But it was his innovation in 1890 which led to the start of a world-dominating label called **REEBOK**…

From household names to words which just can't be forgotten. We have a Bolton man to thank for what is considered to be one of the most well-known quotations in the history of sport. It was Farnworth commentator KENNETH WOLSTENHOLME who said those famous words:

'Some people are on the pitch.
*They think it's all over ... **it is now!'***

BURY

Street lights,
The Old Technical
School
Shuttestock/
Alastair Wallace

Say the name 'Bury' and many people think of **Black Pudding**. Not only because Bury is thought to be the birthplace of the meaty delicacy, but also because of the unusual competition which takes place in Bury every year. In the **World Black Pudding Throwing Championships**, contestants must hurl the pudding at Yorkshire puddings … But don't worry, you don't have to have a good throwing arm to enjoy the local favourite Bury Black Pudding. You can simply buy it as a takeaway snack, best enjoyed hot. You're sure to find this treat at Bury's famous market. The thrice weekly market is now a Bury institution and firm favourite with many shoppers.

Words associated with Bury range all the way from pudding to paper. Paper production has long been a part of the place's history. Bury was the home of many big companies that once kept the nation in this everyday essential. While many of them have since closed down, Bury's fortunes in the world of paper are rising once again with new investments in local factories and thriving paper mills, particularly in places such as Ramsbottom and Radcliffe.

ROCHDALE
Rochdale is known as 'the birthplace of co-operation'. This isn't simply because local people are nice to each other. It's a description based on historical fact. Rochdale is quite literally

where the Co-operative movement started and where that household name The Co-op, had its first start. It was all thanks to the courage and initiative of the Rochdale Pioneers. Back in 1844, they opened their shop to sell good, locally produced food at fair prices. Fast forward to the present day and The Co-operative is an international network offering a huge range of services. Not bad for a group of idealistic hard workers from Rochdale. But Rochdale isn't just known as the birthplace of cooperation. Its geographical location means that it is also sometimes known as 'the backbone of England'.

Rochdale, Number One Riverside Shutterstock/Alastair Wallace

STOCKPORT

Bonnet, headgear, helmet… whatever you call yours, Stockport is closely connected with hats. This is thanks to its past position right at the heart of the UK's hatting industry. While Stockport stopped producing hats in the 1990s, its heritage is celebrated in what is the UK's only museum dedicated to the hatting industry, hats and headwear! Stockport was also the starting point for a famous sporting brand. It is the birthplace of **FRED PERRY** who, after becoming a Wimbledon champion, gave his name to what is now a well-known sports clothing line.

OLDHAM

What is Oldham's connection with one of this country's most well-known politicians? **WINSTON CHURCHILL** was once the Member of Parliament for Oldham in 1900. Oldham also made history in 1978 when it became the birthplace of the first 'test tube' baby, **LOUISE BROWN**.

TAMESIDE

Tameside's name is closely connected with three footballing stars. One is **SIR GEOFF HURST**, who scored a hat-trick for England in 1966, and the second is **SIMONE PERROTTA** who won the World Cup with Italy in 2006, but was born in Ashton-under-Lyne. The third, **JIMMY ARMFIELD**, born in Denton, was captain of England before **BOBBY MOORE** and won 43 caps. While Jimmy wasn't involved in the 1966 World Cup Final performance, he did gain a winner's medal as part of the squad.

TRAFFORD

The history of Trafford is inseparable from that of the Manchester Ship Canal, which went on to shape industry in Greater Manchester for so many years. This association with enterprise continues to this day with household names such as **THE BROOKE BOND TEA COMPANY** and **KELLOGG'S** being based in the area.

SALFORD

Salford is not only closely connected with 'matchstick men' artist **L.S. LOWRY**. It has a rich history in many other ways too, such as its identity as the very first municipal authority to create not just a library but a museum and art gallery in its town. Salford Docks is Manchester rhyming slang for socks, but it's also the name of the docks which were essential to the industry of Manchester and which are now key to tourism and culture in the area. If you're a fan of sport then you may well have heard of the local team doing great things in rugby football, the Salford Reds. Salford became the home of many BBC departments in 2011 when MediaCity was created in what was described by the Director of BBC North, **PETER SALMON**, as 'the biggest move in British broadcasting history'.

Salford Quays Shutterstock/Alastair Wallace

Past Words on Greater Manchester

Life in Greater Manchester has changed a great deal, as the following writings reveal…

From *Folk songs and folk-speech of Lancashire: on the ballads and songs of the county Palatine* by WILLIAM E.A. AXON, published 1871

The Greenside Wakes Song is not much more modern than the days of TIM BOBBIN. Greenside is a small hamlet near Droylsden, and this wakes custom was imported about 1814, from Woodhouses, 'where it had been prevalent for more than the third of a century'. Two men, one of them being dressed to represent a woman, rode in a ceremonious manner, each of them spinning flax, and engaged in a dialogue, which shows the progress and amicable winding up of a domestic dispute as to their relative skill. This song has been printed with the music in CHAMBERS'S Book of Days, as well as in MR. HARLAND'S volume, from which we now quote it:

Droylsden Wakes Song

He:
It's Dreighlsdin Tvakes, im wey're comin' to teawn,
To tell to o' sometliin' o' great reneawn.

Un if this owd jade nil lem'mi begin,
Aw'l show yo how hard un how fast aw con spin.

Chorus:
So its threedywheel, threedywheel, dan, don, dill, doe.

She:
Theaw brags o' thisel, bur aw dunno think it's true,
For aw will uphowd thi, thy fawts arn't a few,
For when theaw hast done, un spun very hard,
O' this awm weel sure, thi wark is marr'd.

So its threedywheel, &c.

He:
Theaw saucy owd jade, theaws'dt best howd thi tung,
Or else awst be thumpin thi ere it be lung,
Un iy 'ot aw do, theawrt sure for to rue,
For aw con ha' monny o one as good as you.

So its threedywheel, &c.

She:
Whot is it to me whoe yo con have?
Aw shanno be lung ere aw'm laid i' my grave;
Un when ut aw'm deod, un have done what aw con,

Yo may foind one ot'll spin as hard as aw've done.

So its threedywheel, &c.

He:
Com, com, mi dear woife, aw'll not ha' thi rue,
Un this aw will tell yo, an aw'll tell yo true,
Neaw if yo'll forgie me for what aw have said,
Aw'll do my endavur to pleos yo instead.
So its threedywheel, &c.

She.
Aw'm glad for to yeor 'ot yo win me forgive,
Un aw will do by yo as long as aw live j
So let us unite, an live free fro o' sin,
Un then we shall have nowt to think at but spin.

So its threedywheel, &c.

Both:
So neaw let's conclude an here eendeth our sung,
Aw hope it has pleost this numerous throng.
Bur iv it 'os mist, yo neednt to fear,
Wey'll do eawr endevur to pleos yo next year.

So its threedywheel, threedywheel, dan, don, dill doe.

Chirrup by EDWIN WAUGH

Young Chirrup wur a mettled cowt:
His heart an' limbs wur true;
At foot race, or at wrostlin'-beawt,
Or aught he buckled to;
At wark or play, reet gallantly
He laid into his game:
An' he're very fond o' singin'-brids –
That's heaw he geet his name.

He're straight as ony pickin'-rod,
An' limber as a snig;
An' th' heartist cock o' th' village clod,
At every country rig:
His shinin' een wur clear an' blue;
His face wur frank an' bowd;
An' th' yure abeawt his monly broo
Wur crisp t i' curls o' gowd.

Young Chirrup donned his clinker't shoon,
An' startin' off to th' fair,
He swore by th' leet o' th' harvest moon,
He'd have a marlock there;
He poo'd a sprig fro th' hawthorn -tree,
That blossomed by the way: –
'Iv ony mon says wrang to me,
Aw'll tan his hide to-day!'

From *Memorials of Old Lancashire* by HENRY FISHWICK, published 1909

Many other poetical works were produced by the pen of MR SKELTON – the largest being of 200 quarto pages, entitled 'The Gleaner', printed by Thos. Cunliffe, of Oxford Street, Bolton, in 1876. There were 1,000 copies struck off. The author, some eight years after, laments its non-success (from a pecuniary point of view) in rhyme, which was sarcastically headed, 'Once I Wrote a Book'. One verse of this will suffice to show the author's sentiments regarding public patronage in matters of published poems:

Once I Wrote a Book
Once I wrote a book
(As at first I hinted),
And direct'y took
It, and got it printed.
But I shall be reckoned
Considerably 'greener'
Ere I print the second
Volume of 'The Gleaner'
And I'll tell you why.
In a quiet way, sir:
Rhyming's 'all my eye',
When it doesn't pay, sir.

CELIA FIENNES

In the time of William and Mary (1689–1694), CELIA FIENNES, sister of the third Viscount Saye and Sele, rode on horseback through some parts of the county, and left a record of the then appearance of some of the towns which are worth repeating.

WIGAN

Wiggons [Wigan] is another pretty market town built of stone and brick, here it is that the fine Channell Coales are in perfection. Of this coale they make saltcellars, stand-dishes and many boxes and things wch are sent about for curiosities and sold in London and are often offer'd in the Exchange in company wth white and black marble and most people deceived by them wch have not been in these countreys and know it ... I bought some of them.

ROCHDALE

I went to an acquaintances house Mr. Taylor and was Civilly Entertained. There is a good Large Meeteing place well filled; these parts Religion does better flourish than in places where they have better advantages.

MANCHESTER

Looks exceedingly well at the Entrance: very substantiall buildings the houses are not very lofty, but mostly of brick and stone, the old houses are timber work [the church, college, and library are described] . . . the market place is large, it takes up two streetes Length when the Market is kept for their Linnen Cloth, Cottontickings wch is the manufacture of the town. This is a thriving place.

Salford's Ancient Ford by H.T CROFTON

Tymology tells us that the town of Salford took its name from a ford, but the ford has long since ceased to exist, and at some distant date a bridge superseded it. There was a bridge between Manchester and Salford so far back as 1226, when a rent of twelve pence was paid for 'a toft in Salford by the bridge' (Lancashire Inquisitions, Record Society, p. 138). This was prior to 1230, about which date Salford received its first charter, and three-quarters of a century before the first charter was granted to Manchester. The thirteenth century was one of considerable progress in the two towns.

From *Bolton bibliography, and jottings of book-lore; with notes on local authors and printers,* by JAMES CHRISTOPHER SCHOLES, published 1886

A first for Bolton

In 1866, JOHN TILLOTSON was joined in partnership by his eldest son, WILLIAM FREDERIC, who on the 19th March, 1867, started the Bolton Evening News, which was the first

English halfpenny evening paper published daily.

Royal Oak Day

Pat had spent some time in what was then – over 90 years ago – best known as the 'Market-town of Bolton', and consequently relates his remembrances about the same, which might well be grouped amongst the collection of Lancashire folk-lore. A custom prevailed, until recent years, of annually celebrating the Royal Oak Day in the township of Tong; this being a day of great rejoicing, it took the form of wakes or fair – for which Lancashire is still universally signalized. The one in question being locally known as 'Turn Fowt Fair'. Here a dummy King Charles was inserted in an old oak tree after being carried in procession round the neighbourhood to the great delight and rejoicings of both old and young. To this ancient custom a few lines are devoted:

'I have,' quoth Pat, 'Tong Fold's gay fair explor'd
To celebrate the second Charles restor'd;
The loj'al youthful crowd with rapture goes
To rouse the monarch from his annual doze
Who peaceful slept, in lofty hay-roost laid,
Disturb'd to be with oumberous pomp array'd,
And borne aloft, the long procession leads
Of flowery garlands and of buxom maids;

In reverend oak they fix his highness' grace.
Where scarce the leaves conceal his sacred face;
In solemn state he o'er the crowd appears.
Nor frowns nor smiles the royal visage wears.'

This Hibernian character [i.e. the character in Scholes's book] is also made to describe another old local pastime, which, after a discontinuance of nearly a century, has been rekindled (with an essential modification), and is now, probably, in the zenith of its popularity, i.e., the game of Football. The only alteration of any moment is the prohibition of the game being played in the public streets, as was customary at the time of which Orrell wrote. In answer to the Bard, the patriot replies:

'If thou one wild audacious sport didst see.
The mighty mob appears as fierce as we,
Where each with lofty look the law disdains,
For once I saw the bold Boltonian swains.
With wooden shoes, with iron plated strong.
Fierce o'er the rattling pavement roll along;
A bladder pent within a leathern case
Was toss'd aluft, a smile array'd each face.
There might'st thou see some hero rush along.
Chief of his party, agile, bold, and strong;
With such a force he kicks the bounding ball.

His footing fails, and earth receives his fall;
But from his downfal quick, with force alert.
He rises in the dignity of dirt.'

The Song of Solomon in the Lancashire Accent as spoken in Bolton by JAMES TAYLOR STATON, published in 1859

The Sung O' Solomon

Chapter I

TH' sung o' sungs, which is Solomon's.

2   *Let him kiss me wi' th' kissins uv his meawth; for thy love's better nur woine.*

3   *Because oth' savvur o' thy good eighntments thy name's as eighntment temm'd forth, theerefore do th' varjuns love thee.*

4   *Poo me, we'll run after thee: th' king's browt me into his reawms: we'll be fain un rejeighce in thee, we'll think o' thy love mooar nur woine: th' upreet love thee.*

5   *Awm black, but comely, O yoa dowters o' Jerusalem, as th' tents o' Kedar, as th' curtains o' Solomon.*

6   *Look not uppo me, because awm black, because th' sun's lookt on me: my mother's childer wur vext at me; they made me keeper oth' voineyerds; but my own voineyort have aw not kept.*

7   *Tell me, O theaw uz my sowl loves, wheere theaw feeds, wheere theaw makes thy flocks to rest at noon: for waw should aw be uz one ut turns asoide by th' flocks o' thy companions?*

8   *If theaw doesn't know, O theaw fairest among wimmin, goo thy way forth by th' footsteps oth' flock, un feed thy kids by th' shepherd's tents.*

9   *Awve compared thee, O ma love, to a ruck o' hawses i' Phayroh's chariots.*

10   *Thy cheeks are cumly wi' rows o' jewels, thy neck wi' cheons o' gowd.*

11   *We'll make thee borders o' gowd wi' studs o' silver.*

12   *Whoile th' king keawrs at his table, ma spoikenurt sends forth th' smell theereof*

Happy Birthday, Greater Manchester!

Greater Manchester recently celebrated its 40th birthday as a region! It was on 1 April 1974 that Greater Manchester was officially formed and the ten boroughs, which had formally been part of Cheshire and Lancashire, became one. The boroughs of Salford, Manchester, Bolton, Bury, Trafford, Tameside, Rochdale, Wigan, Stockport and Oldham officially came into being, overseen by Greater Manchester Council and Greater Manchester Police. The new region has an exciting past and present, as shown by the fascinating facts below!

- Greater Manchester has a population of around 2.5 million people. That means that more people live in Greater Manchester than in Kosovo or Johannesburg.

- Greater Manchester has four professional orchestras.

- Before 1974, Wigan was one of only four royal boroughs in the county.

- Manchester airport is the third busiest in the UK.

- Greater Manchester has the highest number of theatre seats per head of population outside London.

- The county's average annual rainfall is 806.6

millimetres compared to the UK average of 1,125 millimetres.

• Greater Manchester is the only place in the UK to have a fully orbital motorway, the M60, which passes through eight of the boroughs. (London's M25 does not make a full orbit because the Dartford crossing is the A282).

• Before the metropolitan county was created, the name SELNEC was used for the area. This is from the initials of 'South East Lancashire North East Cheshire'.

• When the boroughs were formed in 1974, Salford was nearly named Irwell, but the name was changed after protests that the River Irwell flowed through two other boroughs but did not run through Worsley.

• Cheshire and Lancashire used to be separated by the River Mersey.

• No fewer than twenty Nobel prize winners have come from Greater Manchester!

• Greater Manchester is the third most visited place in the UK and the second in England, after London.

- Football brought in around £330 million worth of economic benefit to Greater Manchester in 2013 alone!

- Manchester is the largest of the ten Greater Manchester Authorities with a population of almost 500,000 people.

- On 26 September 1916, Bolton became the target for one of the first aerial offensives in history. A Zeppelin of the Imperial German Navy dropped 21 bombs on the town.

- In 2007, the Church of Scientology bought the Old Trafford Essence Distillery on Chester Road and planned to turn it into a place of worship and religious instruction. The plans were rejected by Trafford Council.

- The reason so many locals still use Cheshire/Lancashire in their address is that Greater Manchester wasn't added as a Royal Mail postal county until 1996!

Page opposite: The Beetham Tower, the tallest skyscraper in Manchester
©Andy & Sue Caffrey